LEARNING TO PRAY

"The potency of prayer hath subdued the strength of fire; it hath bridled the rage of lions, hushed anarchy to rest, extinguished wars, appeased the elements, expelled the demons, burst the chains of death, expanded the gates of heaven, assuaged diseases, repelled frauds, rescued cities from destruction, stayed the sun in its course, and arrested the progress of the thunderbolt. Prayer is all-efficient panoply, a treasure undiminished, a mine which is never exhausted, a sky unobscured by clouds, a heaven unruffled by storm. It is the root, the fountain, the mother of a thousand blessings."

~ Chrysostom

LEARNING TO
PRAY

K.P. Yohannan

BOOKS

a division of Gospel for Asia

www.gfa.org

Learning to Pray

ISBN: 978-1-59589-029-0

Published by gfa books, a division of Gospel for Asia
1800 Golden Trail Court, Carrollton, TX 75010 USA
phone: (972) 300-7777
fax: (972) 300-7778

Printed in the United States

For information about other materials, visit our website:
www.gfa.org.

07 08 09 10 11 12 / 6 5 4 3

Table of Contents

Introduction

How often have you heard someone say, "I will pray for you" or ask, "Please pray for me"? Of the thousands of letters I receive, a significant number of them always have some kind of prayer request included.

The need for prayer is felt in all aspects of our lives. Whether it has to do with our families, children, education, daily needs, ministry, relatives, friends or the many other concerns that can fill our days, the necessity of prayer is always present.

But despite that, the question remains: Do we honestly take time to pray? If we do pray, how much time do we really spend in prayer? We may spend hours each day talking to friends and family members about the things in our lives, but do we even spend at least one hour with the Lord in prayer, talking with Him?

I believe our lack of prayer is because so few of us truly know how to pray. I know that in the early days of my Christian life, I had no clue what prayer really was. I would close my eyes, and in a few short minutes, I would run out of things to say. It wasn't until learning from older brothers and sisters in Christ, as well as from books on prayer, especially those of E.M. Bounds, that I began to grow in my prayer life.

May this booklet serve to give you the beginning steps for building your life on the solid foundation of prayer. And may the Lord use this to help you come near to Him and be a child again, simply talking to your Father. He is waiting for you.

CHAPTER ONE

A Secret Foundation

A few years ago, I heard the story of one missionary serving with our organization who, in a short time, had planted five churches in a difficult part of Northeast India. Curious of how this young brother did it, I called one of our senior leaders and asked him if he could tell me more about this brother's ministry.

All that I knew was that he was from a tribal background and didn't have any college education, yet regardless, it seemed that God was with him in a remarkable way. The first church he planted began with the healing of a Hindu priest who was paralyzed. Then, one after another, four more churches were born.

I was more than curious to find out this brother's secret.

Our senior leader said he would check into it and let me know what he found out. When he called to tell me, he said, "There is nothing unusual about him. I found nothing special except for one thing—he gets up very early each morning and spends two or three hours in prayer and then an hour or two reading the Bible. This habit began while he was studying in one of our Bible colleges."

Let me give another example. One morning I was talking to a senior leader in our work on the mission field. He was traveling throughout North India to meet with many of our leaders and appoint new workers to projects that had recently been started. In our conversation we were discussing who might be able to take a certain new position. I asked him, "What do you think about this particular brother? He seems to be a really godly man. Why don't we think about putting him in that position?"

We talked back and forth about this brother's abilities, his lack of experience and the seriousness of the challenge in this new area of work. But finally we both agreed to trust him with the particular job. There was something about him that caused us to make that decision: He spends nearly four hours in prayer each day.

Our decision was not based on the fact that he had started a dozen churches or that he was able to oversee a large region of the country quite well. Our decision was based on the fact that God was with him and that he knew how to pray.

You see, prayer is God's method of carrying out His purposes upon this earth. There is a mystery to the truth that God waits to hear and answer the prayers of His people. Remember what Jesus said in Matthew 9:37–38? "The harvest truly is plentiful, but the laborers are few. *Therefore pray* the Lord of the harvest to send out laborers into His harvest" (emphasis added).

There are many people all throughout Christian history who knew the power of prayer. John Hyde was one of them. In the late 1800s, he left his home in Illinois to serve the Lord as a missionary to the people of India. There he labored, not just physically but, more important, in prayer. He was known to stay up late into the night praying, as well as rising very early each morning, crying out to God, "Give me souls, O God, or I die!" He was so gripped with passion for the lost, and he knew that the strongholds the enemy had upon the people could only be broken through prayer. And so pray he did.

In fact, he prayed so much that the position of his heart shifted in his chest, later causing the complications that led to his death. But because of his prayers, in 1904 the northwestern states of India where he had labored for years experienced one of the greatest revivals the nation has ever known!

Just like Praying Hyde, we too can learn to pray and see God accomplish great things through our prayers. But we must learn. We could read every book ever written on prayer, but that won't make us people of prayer. We learn to pray by doing it.

In *The Last Days Newsletter,* Leonard Ravenhill tells about a group of tourists who were visiting a picturesque village. As they walked by an old man sitting beside a fence, one tourist, in a rather patronizing way, turned to the old man and asked, "Were any great men born in this village?" The old man simply turned and replied, "Nope, only babies."

My brothers and sisters, we must *grow* into the life of prayer. Let us begin today, taking the first steps toward becoming people great in prayer. As we do, we will see incredible things happen in our lifetime. "The earnest prayer of a righteous person has great power and wonderful results" (James 5:16, NLT).

I know firsthand just how effective the prayers of those who trust the Lord and continue in prayer are. For three and one-half years my mother fasted and prayed for the Lord to call one of her six sons into full-time ministry. One after the other, each of my brothers started their careers, with only me, the youngest and shyest, left as my mother's last hope.

But when I was 16, the Lord answered my mother's prayers and called me to the ministry. The call on my life is a direct result of her prayers.

As John Wesley once said, "God will do nothing but in answer to prayer."[1]

I believe John Wesley first learned the importance of prayer and how to pray through the example he saw in his mother, Susanna Wesley. This woman of God and mother of 19 children was known for her devoted prayer life. In the midst of her busy household and numerous duties, she consistently made time to pray by pulling her apron over her head to find solitude with God. It was out of her prayers that two of her sons—John and Charles Wesley—became key leaders in the Church in the 1700s.

"Call to Me, and I will answer you, and show you great and mighty things, which you do not know" (Jeremiah 33:3). Let us receive

His invitation and begin to walk this road of learning to pray.

CHAPTER TWO

What Is Prayer?

If you've had similar experiences as I, you may have found how oftentimes in prayer, either public or private, people change their voices and stretch their words, as if talking to some unknown, powerful being a million light years away. Their voice may fluctuate and they may sound as though they were giving a speech or trying to convince God to do something. This, my brothers and sisters, is not to be defined as prayer.

Contrary to a lot of religious examples, prayer need not be just some mystical, super-spiritual activity. Simply put, prayer is conversation between Father and child.

Have you ever noticed how a child comes and talks to his mom or dad? You never need to look for a dictionary to find out the meaning of the words children use. They come just as they are. They come simply. You will never find a child getting into a frenzy and fluctuating his voice as he talks. All you will hear is a small voice, in simple conversation, looking up into the mom's or dad's eyes.

One of the most exhilarating experiences for me is when I get a chance to hear a little child pray. It will make you both laugh and cry at the same time. Read some of these prayers from children:

Dear Lord,
Thank you for the nice day today. You even fooled the TV weatherman.
Hank (age 7)

Dear Lord,
Do you ever get mad? My mother gets mad all the time but she is only human.
Yours truly,
David (age 8)

Dear Lord,
I need a raise in my allowance. Could you have one of your angels tell my father?
Thank you,
David (age 7)[1]

In Matthew 18:3, Jesus turned to the disciples gathered around Him and taught them an important lesson: "Unless you . . . become as little children, you will by no means enter the kingdom of heaven." The way a child prays, in simplicity and trust, is the perfect portrait of prayer.

When we look at the prayer of Jesus in John 17, we find the same picture. Jesus didn't close His eyes and pray in a different tone of voice. In fact, we are told that "Jesus . . . *lifted up His eyes* to heaven, and said: *'Father'* " (John 17:1, emphasis added).

What a beautiful portrait of His relationship with the Father! Through this example, Jesus was showing us that prayer is simply talking to God—not just as the almighty Creator of the universe, but as the caring, lovesick Father who waits for His child to come, a Father who delights to be with His children.

Come Just as You Are to the Father

We have need to remember this through our days. So easily we can forget that the Father loves us just as He loved Jesus. Then, instead of coming to Him because of who He is, we are kept at bay, consumed more with who we are or are not.

I believe the enemy has numerous tactics to keep us from praying because he knows that it is the greatest way for the kingdom of God to expand. He also understands how our hearts and perspective on the situations of life are changed through prayer.

Perhaps you are one who truly desires to pray, yet when you do, you are soon bogged down with all the ways you fail, remembering how you aren't matching up to the spiritual person you want to be, until eventually all motivation to pray is lost in guilt.

Our Father in heaven knows us. And I believe that is why Jesus told the parable of the prodigal son in Luke 15. Although it is often taught with the emphasis being on the prodigal son, I believe Jesus was trying more to paint a clear picture of our God and *Father*.

> He [the prodigal son] arose and came to his father. But when he was still a great way off, his father saw him and had compassion, and ran and fell on his neck and kissed him. And the son said to him, "Father, I have sinned against heaven and in your sight, and am no longer worthy to be called your son."
>
> But the father said to his servants, "Bring out the best robe and put it on him, and put a ring on his hand and

sandals on his feet. And bring the fatted
calf here and kill it, and let us eat and be
merry; for this my son was dead and is
alive again; he was lost and is found." And
they began to be merry (Luke 15:20–24).

I share this with you because I know how
easily guilt can keep us from talking with
our Father. Please see how the father *rejoiced*
at his son's return. Instead of reprimanding
him, punishing him, demanding he say sorry
or make some sort of restitution, the father
embraced his son, *rejoiced* and even *called for
a celebration.* Remember this promise: "There
is therefore now no condemnation to those
who are in Christ Jesus" (Romans 8:1).

> For we do not have a High Priest who
> cannot sympathize with our weaknesses,
> but was in all points tempted as we are,
> yet without sin. Let us therefore *come
> boldly to the throne of grace,* that we may
> obtain mercy and find grace to help in
> time of need (Hebrews 4:15–16, empha-
> sis added).

So then, let us pray, remembering who
it is we call Father and realizing that prayer
is coming to Him and listening to what He
has to say. Prayer is waiting before Him and
meditating long enough in His presence until
our hearts are touched and moved with His

concerns and burdens, so that we become channels for Him to work through.

Prayer is our willingness to say no to our own desires and accept suffering in the flesh, to experience the pain and agony the Lord feels for the events and people in our generation.

Prayer is our willingness to join with the unseen Christ in the Garden of Gethsemane and experience His pain and heartbreak for a world that is lying in utter darkness, plunging into eternity to perish forever.

Prayer is standing in the gap on behalf of the needy and hurting, asking the Father to heal and to save before it is too late (see Ezekiel 22:30).

E.M. Bounds said it perfectly: "Prayer is the outstretched arms of the child for the Father's help."[2]

The Nearness of God

So then we see that prayer has less to do with words and posture and more to do with intimacy and closeness, like a child has with his father or mother.

The nearness of God is not determined by space and time, but rather by the inner relationship and intimate fellowship we have with Him in our hearts.

Just the other day, I was meeting with a

few of my coworkers in the ministry. Before we started to discuss some things we were dealing with, I said, "Let us pray."

Gathered in my office and sitting in our chairs, I began to pray, "Lord, You are the One who promised that when we gather like this You will be with us. Right now we are here because of You and in Your name. We are Your sons and daughters."

All of a sudden, I felt like we should have another chair in the room because Jesus was certainly present with us. In my mind, I did not want Jesus standing somewhere while we were all sitting down. You see, in my Asian culture, it is terribly impolite and unacceptable for a subordinate to sit while there is a superior standing. This is why when a superior walks into a room everyone stands up until the superior sits down and asks for everyone else to please sit as well. This thought came to my mind, and I prayed right in the middle of it, "Lord, I feel like we should have a chair for You because You are right here with us." In fact, Jesus assured us that "where two or three are gathered together in My name, I am there in the midst of them" (Matthew 18:20).

In all of our prayers, whether private or public, let us have this attitude and frame of reference for sharing our prayer: We are talking to a Father who is closer to us than our own thoughts. He is near, so near that no words can describe it.

In Psalm 73, we read of a godly man who, in the midst of tremendous discouragement and inner struggles, finally recognized the nearness of God. After all was said and done, he cried out saying, "The nearness of God is my good" (Psalm 73:28, NASB). His prayer is no longer directed to somebody far away, but to someone who is near to him. It is the understanding of this that changed his view on the situations of his life and even changed his own heart.

Let us then remember that when we pray there is no reason we should close our eyes and imagine some strange being far away. Rather, let us have the honest attitude of a little child talking to his father.

I believe the Lord is so delighted when we approach Him with a childlike heart, sharing our concerns and burdens with Him in this manner.

> Tell God all that is in your heart, as one
> unloads one's heart, its pleasures and
> its pains, to a dear friend. Tell Him your
> troubles, that He may comfort you; tell
> Him your joys, that He may sober them;
> tell Him your longings, that He may
> purify them; tell Him your dislikes, that
> He may help you to conquer them; talk

to Him of your temptations, that He may shield you from them; show Him the wounds of your heart, that He may heal them; lay bare your indifference to good, your depraved tastes for evil, your instability. Tell Him how self-love makes you unjust to others, how vanity tempts you to be insincere, how pride disguises you to yourself and others.

If you thus pour out all your weakness, needs, troubles, there will be no lack of what to say. You will never exhaust the subject. It is continually being renewed. People who have no secrets from each other never want for subject of conversation. They do not weigh their words, for there is nothing to be held back; neither do they seek for something to say. They talk out of the abundance of the heart, without consideration they say just what they think. Blessed are they who attain to such familiar, unreserved intercourse with God.[3]

CHAPTER THREE

Foundations in Prayer

God has of His own motion placed
Himself under the law of prayer, and has
obligated Himself to answer the prayers of
men. He has ordained prayer as a means
whereby He will do things through men
as they pray, which He would not other-
wise do. . . . If prayer puts God to work
on earth, then, by the same token, prayer-
lessness rules God out of the world's
affairs, and prevents Him from working.[1]

Those words perfectly communicate the
importance of God's people praying.
Prayer is no light thing, yet at the same time
it is simple communication between the

Learning to Pray

Father God and His children, and as E.M. Bounds said in his book *Purpose in Prayer*, "The driving power, the conquering force in God's cause is God Himself. 'Call upon Me and I will answer thee and show thee great and mighty things which thou knowest not,' is God's challenge to prayer. Prayer puts God in full force into God's work."[2]

Let us then receive His challenge and engage ourselves in a life of fervent prayer. For "the effective, fervent prayer of a righteous man avails much" (James 5:16).

Why Should We Pray?

Pray because God tells you to. What more reason do we need? It's a command that we are given over and over again. Luke 18:1 says, "Then He spoke a parable to them, that men always ought to pray and not lose heart." Philippians 4:6 says, "Be anxious for nothing, but in everything by prayer and supplication, with thanksgiving, let your requests be made known to God." Ephesians 6:18 also instructs us to pray. Pray about everything, small things, big things and all things. "Pray without ceasing" (1 Thessalonians 5:17).

Pray because God has promised to answer. If you want to see things accomplished, ask. God says, "Yet you do not have because you do not ask" (James 4:2). Do you want to

see Bhutan, India, Mongolia or some other
nations changed? Do you want to see another
50 people added to the staff of Gospel for
Asia? Do you want to see more workers raised
up on the fields? Do we need funds for vari-
ous projects? Are there dreams and visions
you want fulfilled? You can talk about it all
you want, but it won't happen unless you ask.
Without prayer, nothing of lasting value is
going to happen.

God delights in answering the prayer of
faith. The last part of Hebrews 11:6 says, "He
is a rewarder of those who diligently seek
Him." In Matthew 7:7 Jesus said, "Ask, and it
will be given to you; seek, and you will find;
knock, and it will be opened to you." John
15:7 says, "If you abide in Me, and My words
abide in you, you will ask what you desire,
and it shall be done for you." We are given
this promise over and over again in Scripture.
God answers prayer.

Cornelius, a Gentile, prayed, and God sent
Peter to talk to him (see Acts 10:1–2). God is
eager to answer our cries for help.

Elijah was a man, weak like all of us (see
James 5:17). Yet he prayed that there would
be no rain, and for three and a half years
there was a drought. Then he prayed for rain,
and a storm came.

Daniel prayed, stood firm in his God and

saw the victory (see Daniel 9).

From the belly of the fish Jonah prayed, and God heard him (see Jonah 2:1). Hagar prayed. Moses prayed. God answered them. I think also about people that I know. Our own experiences tell us that God really does answer prayer.

Let me tell you a story from the village in which I was born and raised. One particular year, the entire rice crop was failing. It was a disastrous year for our community. But there was one believer who really trusted the Lord. When the rice crops began to fail, he said, "I belong to the Lord. My field belongs to the Lord. I know the entire community is facing this problem, but I trust my God to take care of my crops." He fasted and prayed; amazingly, God did a miracle that no one could explain. In the midst of thousands of acres of failing rice fields, his five or ten acres were protected.

Week after week at GFA headquarters, we read letters from people who write to us saying, "Would you please pray for this?" We get prayer requests from all over, and we take these requests seriously and pray. Later we hear the praise reports: "Nobody can explain how it happened, but God answered prayer . . . The money that we needed came in . . . We found the perfect individual to do the work . . . The Lord healed him." All kinds of unbelievable things happen when people pray.

Pray because major events must transpire in our lifetime. God wants things to happen. The work's forward progress depends on our praying. It really does. Let this sink in. God really answers prayer. As you ask Him, He answers specifically and miraculously. I have seen it so many times.

Prayer is a sure way to see God do miracles on our behalf. Gideon, Moses, Daniel, Elijah and Paul all prayed, and things happened. Jesus prayed before He raised Lazarus from the dead and before He fed the five thousand. The Bible is filled with people praying and things happening in answer to those prayers. Right now God is waiting to answer the prayers from your lips. Sometimes the answer may take longer in coming, but keep on asking. Keep on seeking. Keep on knocking. God truly answers prayer.

Pray so that your joy may be full. In John 16:24 Jesus said, "Until now you have asked nothing in My name. Ask, and you will receive, that your joy may be full."

Do you want to be full of joy? Then let God show you some answers to prayer. All of us can testify to the joy of answered prayer.

When our children were growing up, we

encouraged them to pray for their needs. One time my son, Daniel, was praying for a particular pair of tennis shoes. A stranger who knew nothing about this prayer bought the exact shoes that Daniel was praying for and gave them to him as a gift. Imagine the joy and the thrill of a young heart experiencing God's answer to prayer! So it is with us as adults too.

Pray because it is the best cure for worry and concerns. When we pray, we leave the matter in God's hands and are free from worry and concern.

Someone once said, "Why pray when you can worry about it?" But Philippians 4:6–7 says, "Be anxious for nothing, but in everything by prayer and supplication, with thanksgiving, let your requests be made known to God." God has given us the invitation to cast all our cares upon Him, for He cares for us (see 1 Peter 5:7). What is bothering you? Please, just pray. When you are troubled about anything, pray.

Pray because it makes our God happy. Hebrews 11:6 tells us, "Without faith it is impossible to please Him." It brings joy to the heart of God when we turn to Him in prayer, depending on Him to move in the circumstances of our lives.

How Should We Pray?

Pray with absolute confidence that God is on our side. When we pray, the devil will bombard us and make us feel sinful and horrible about ourselves. We will never come to the place of being holy enough for God to hear our prayer. Rather, we stand before the Lord pure, transparent and righteous because it is a gift He has given us through His Son. It is not something we can earn. We are the righteousness of God in Christ Jesus. It is nothing we attain. It is only by grace that we are children of God. As we come to Him and say "Father," He truly is our Father. He is our confidence.

He answers prayer not based on how great or mighty or holy we are. No. It is His grace. "[Nothing] shall be able to separate us from the love of God which is in Christ Jesus our Lord" (Romans 8:39). This truth needs to be drilled into our hearts and minds if we are to have a confident, effective prayer life.

Pray with a thankful heart. Be committed to thank Him for what He has done, for who He is and for what He will do. Praise Him. Give Him glory. Say, "Lord, let Your name be praised. Hallowed be Thy name. May Your name be lifted up."

When you come before the Lord, look back and see what He has already done for you and thank Him for all that. Look forward also to see what the Lord has promised to do and thank Him in advance for what He will do.

Pray remembering your relationships with others. "And forgive us our debts, as we forgive our debtors" (Matthew 6:12). When you pray, make sure there is no bitterness, anger or unforgiveness in your heart toward anyone. This is very important. If you have these sort of feelings, ask the Lord to give you true forgiveness and love for the individual. Ask the Lord to help you love him as He loves him.

Be specific in your prayers. Matthew 6:11 says, "Give us this day . . ." Ask Him for exactly what you need. What do you need today to sustain His work and accomplish His will? Don't pray in general terms. Have specific things that you want God to answer. Tell Him the name and place. Let Him know who, what, where and so forth. Tell God specifically. Don't tell Him how to answer, but be specific in what the needs are.

Pray with a burden. Breakthrough in prayer comes through a heart that has been burdened by the Holy Spirit. Read Nehemiah 1. Nehemiah was so burdened that he could not even regulate his own expression and emotion because of the grief he had over the suffering of God's people.

Study the lives of Hannah, Moses, David and Paul. You will find this passion in their prayers as well. In Ephesians, you read about Paul praying for these people. It's like he is in anguish. He talks about his "tribulations" for them (see Ephesians 3:13). In Galatians he says, "My little children, for whom I labor in birth again until Christ is formed in you" (Galatians 4:19).

How do we get this burden? We simply seek it. We ask God to change our heart. We say, "Lord, what is on Your heart? What is Your concern? Lord, please let me understand it." Then He brings the thoughts and gives us the burden to intercede. We cannot create this burden on our own. God does not care about lip service. He wants us to enter into the reality of what He feels for the suffering humanity all around us. He wants to share with us His burdens and His joy in seeing these prayers answered.

I was in Singapore for a leaders' meeting in 1971. There I heard Dr. Bob Pierce, founder of World Vision, tell of his early years when he visited China. He said that when he saw the multitudes in China, he was broken-hearted. He wept on the streets of that nation. Then he took his Bible and wrote on the leaflet inside, "Let my heart break for the things that break God's heart." Let that be our prayer also.

Pray in faith. We must believe. Jesus said, "Therefore I say to you, whatever things you ask when you pray, believe that you receive them, and you will have them" (Mark 11:24). Matthew 17:19–20 says, "Then the disciples came to Jesus privately and said, 'Why could we not cast it out?' So Jesus said to them, 'Because of your unbelief; for assuredly, I say to you, if you have faith as a mustard seed, you will say to this mountain, "Move from here to there," and it will move; and nothing will be impossible for you.' "

"All things are possible to him who believes" (Mark 9:23). I don't understand how it works, but God said as we pray we must keep believing that He has answered our prayer. The believing comes from Him. He is the author and finisher of our faith (see Hebrews 12:2). Faith is not something we can work up in ourselves. We can't convince ourselves to believe. We have to ask Him for believing faith. The father of the afflicted son did that. He said to Jesus, "Lord, I believe; help my unbelief!" (Mark 9:24).

Pray in the Holy Spirit. Sometimes we don't know how to pray when God lays a burden upon our hearts. But the Holy Spirit can pray through us. It can be in a language that nobody understands. It can be in groanings and cryings too deep for words. Please don't try to figure this out. God is so wonderful that when we don't know how to pray, the

Holy Spirit intercedes through us. When our ability to pray comes to an end, God takes over (see Romans 8:26).

Our God is eager to hear our prayers. Let us then come before Him in the morning, in the evening, while we are waiting in line, driving to work or washing the dishes. Prayer need not be an activity we engage in for only an hour each morning. Rather, let us live in the atmosphere of prayer, our hearts continually being lifted up in prayer to Him. In doing so, we will come to experience the wonder of being colaborers with God as He works through our prayers (see 1 Corinthians 3:9).

CHAPTER FOUR

Prayer in Action

We on the mission field have an aware-
ness that we are on the verge of some
major breakthroughs for the kingdom in
many of the countries in which we are working. We hear statements such as: "Soon the
whole country of Nepal will have a Christian
witness in every village!" "India shall be
saved!" "No matter what, one of these days
Bhutan will be saved!"

Those statements are not made casually.
There is a depth to them because God has
impressed these things on our hearts. Because
of that, we feel the time given to us now should
be filled with prayer and serious commitment
in seeking God for what He wants to do.

Miracles Happen

I will never forget some of the answers to prayer that God has given us. One such incident happened in the early days of our radio listeners' crusade in India. More than 25,000 people had gathered in the meeting place to hear the message that evening. As we were driving toward the meeting place, we saw dark clouds over the town. It was obvious that it could rain at any moment. I thought the meeting was going to have to be called off. But the brother traveling with me in the car said, "Well, Elijah was a man just like us. He prayed and it didn't rain."

When we got to the meeting ground, we could hear the roar of rain in the distance. Then it began to drizzle slightly. I was on the stage as the meeting was just about to start and felt that I should tell the people that Jesus would answer prayer tonight and hold off the rain.

You know, sometimes we pray with unbelief. I prayed that way that evening. I wasn't so sure that the rain really would be held off. But praise God there was prayer going up from other concerned people who did believe.

Would you believe, it was like somebody was holding an umbrella over that ground! In just that meeting place, there was not one drop of rain. Rain was pouring down all around us, but our meeting was dry.

Suppose no one had prayed. It would have been so natural for me to say, "You know, there's no hope. This meeting is rained out. It's not going to work. Let's go home." Suppose no one had believed. I can tell you what would have happened. The whole place would have been flooded. There is no doubt about it. But God gave us the grace to pray and to believe a little bit for the answer. And He did it.

Another illustration of the power of prayer happened some years ago. In our Indian headquarters, the leadership felt the need to really seek the Lord for His guidance. As the Lord burdened our hearts, we called for four days of fasting and prayer. During that time of ministry to the Lord, the Lord spoke to us through one of our brothers. Because of this man's godliness and intimate walk with the Lord, we took the words very seriously. The instruction was that there would be a major investigation from the government with the intention to hinder the ministry. The admonition from the Lord was, "Seek My face. They will come as lions and leave as lambs."

We were all doing well. We had never had any major problems with government authorities before. If it were not for this particular brother's groundedness in the Lord, I would have thought that his imagination was running wild. But we took it seriously and began to pray and ask the Lord to go before us.

As we took the time to seek Him in this, He began to burden our hearts with specific things to pray. We knew the Lord was calling us to stand in the gap with prayer for the ministry more than ever before. Ezekiel 22:30 became a key verse for us: "So I sought for a man among them who would make a wall, and stand in the gap before Me on behalf of the land, that I should not destroy it; but I found no one."

If you read the rest of that chapter, you will find that the people did not take seriously the call to pray. It was in God's power to save that nation, but because no one prayed, they were destroyed.

So we prayed. Some weeks went by, and suddenly we got a letter from the government, saying, "Seven of us are coming. We'll be there in five days. We are coming to study and investigate your organization." At the bottom of the letter was a man's signature. When we read the name, we were all scared. This man was a very well-known, righteous Brahmin and a high government official. We knew they had the ability to hinder us in the ministry. But because of the word from the

Lord and the prayer that came from that, we were prepared.

Sure enough, at the time designated, this official came with his people and stayed several days at our office. They went through all our books and records. They studied the way we worked. They asked question after question. It was clear that they were trying to find out if we had broken any laws, misused funds or were doing anything to hurt the government in any way.

I'll never forget the day these men left. I had a brief talk with the head official as he left our office building. He turned to me and said, "I came with the intention of sealing your doors and closing down your organization. Looking at the expanse of the ministry, I could not convince myself things could be right. But I can tell you, I've never been to one institution that is so upright. I can't find a single thing that is even questionable."

We continued talking, and he began to tell me his life story. During the Pakistan-India division in 1947, he ended up in Pakistan but soon escaped to India. He worked as a coolie in the railway station, got himself into the university and then became one of the highest government officials.

As our conversation came to an end, he said, "Would you pray for me? I'm not well.

My back is hurting all the time." This devout Hindu knelt and asked me to lay my hand on him and pray for him! Then he said, "If I can ever do anything to help you and your people, please contact me."

Through this whole process, we remembered the word the Lord had spoken to us earlier: "Seek My face. They will come as lions and leave as lambs." The first two or three days, the investigators were not friendly and very suspicious. But just as the Lord had spoken, they left smiling and as wonderful friends.

This was one of those experiences that the Lord allowed us to go through to teach us that if we walk with Him, He will guide us. His work is not a business. It is not something in which we plan, scheme and work out the details. He is teaching us to be child-like so that He can instruct us and lead us as we seek His face. That is just one of the many, many experiences that have shown us the importance of being led by Him and the power of prayer.

No Magic Formula

People often ask about our organization. They want to know how we do things. They want to know how we run a particular part of the ministry or how we handle a certain kind of problem. They are seeking to figure out the reason for our success and growth. But there is no magic formula. All I can do is encourage them with how the organization began with prayer and continues with prayer.

Sometimes these people call us back and say, "Yes, prayer, but what else?" All I can tell them is, "We didn't know what we were doing most of the time and we still don't. We go along as the Lord guides and leads us. We make mistakes, we change things and we go on seeking His face. I do not know any magic formula."

In all the 25 years of this ministry, every major breakthrough we have seen in the work has come through prayer. Through prayer, we let God be God, yielding ourselves as earthen vessels and becoming channels for His work. I am deeply convinced that the shortest route to getting things done is by prayer.

On the other hand, my nature is opposed to this. I want to make changes and get things accomplished. I like to think and say, "If we don't do this or that, it isn't going to happen." But then I remember that every failure we have had and every setback we have experienced was always because we calculated and did something out of careful planning, but not careful prayer.

Why did the Lord caution the Ephesian

Church in Revelation 2 that He might remove their lampstand from its place? Why, in spite of their sound doctrine and hard work for Him, was Christ grieved? What was it that the Lord saw that caused Him to say that they had left their first love?

The answer is found in how the Ephesians became self-sufficient in their own eyes. Their reputation, money, resources, expertise and carefully planned strategies caused them to rely on themselves. They began to think that they no longer needed to come to Him, to fellowship with Him or to depend on Him.

Our praying speaks of our ever-present need for the Lord and shows how much we truly depend on Him. Only through prayer will we accomplish His purposes.

In *The Reality of Prayer*, E.M. Bounds says, "Nonpraying is lawlessness, discord, anarchy. Prayer, in the moral government of God, is as strong and far-reaching as the law of gravitation in the material world, and it is as necessary as gravitation to hold things in their proper sphere and in life."[1] There is no magic formula; there is only the absolute necessity of prayer.

The most efficient and effective way—the only way—to see the things around us change and His purposes come about is to depend on Him in prayer.

CHAPTER FIVE

Now Begin

Now after reading many stories of answered prayer, perhaps you are beginning to realize in a new way the power of prayer, the many reasons to pray and what the attitudes of your heart should be as you pray. Maybe now you are inspired to pray in new ways than before and are very encouraged in your heart. But unless you go one step further, this inspiration will amount to absolutely nothing.

You must begin to pray. All the understanding about prayer, all the excitement about praying more and all the good intentions in the world are completely useless, unless you pray.

Practical Suggestions for Individual Prayer

I want to make you aware of some things that are helpful to keep in mind regarding prayer.

Develop the discipline of prayer. First of all, you must realize Satan knows that prayer is the fastest way to advance the kingdom of God. Therefore, he will try everything he possibly can to stop you from praying. He will even prompt you to do "good things" to replace time spent in prayer.

At times prayer will come naturally, with little effort. But at other times, it will be a struggle to get your mind and will in gear to pray. Prayer is a spiritual discipline. Please, do not be discouraged when you feel like you are fighting upstream in prayer. Realize that it is hard because it truly is the most significant thing you could be doing. It is worth the fight. Keep in the battle.

And just as we discussed that prayer acknowledges our dependence on the Lord, it applies even in the very area of praying. Ask the Lord for His help to pray and to know how to pray. Tell Him, "Lord, I really desire to pray as You would like; please help me to pray." He most definitely will help you. Make this your daily prayer and truly depend on Him for His help to guide you. I guarantee you will see your prayer life grow.

Take it step by step. Oftentimes, not knowing how to practically start praying regularly
stops people from beginning to develop
their prayer life. Because they are not sure
when to pray, how long to pray, what to pray
for, if they should have a list of daily prayer
requests or simply seek to hear what the
Lord is saying each day, the act of praying is
delayed until it eventually becomes nonexis-
tent. If this is you, take time to hear what the
Lord is saying for you to do right now. We
learn step by step, little by little. Take those
steps today.

We must make sure that we do not con-
coct our own prayer life, but rather are led by
the Lord in all things. Maybe you would like
to pray for three hours a day, but it could be
the Lord wants you first to be faithful with
a smaller amount. It could be that as you
continue to seek Him for how He wants you
to pray, He will move it up until you can be
faithful to pray for three hours a day.

Or it could be that He just wants you to be
faithful to pray for one need right now until
that prayer is answered. Or He may desire
that each day you listen to hear from Him
afresh, understanding what is on His heart for
the day. The Lord will show you as you seek
Him. Be faithful with whatever He shows you,
and you will see a difference. Prayer is more

about hearing than about verbalizing. As you seek to hear what the Lord desires and you do it, you will see your life transformed.

Pray with others. One thing that I have found significant throughout my years of knowing the Lord is the incredible encouragement it is to pray *with* others. Many times, joining in prayer with a friend has served as not only an encouragement, but also an exciting journey on which we together see the Lord move in incredible ways through the things we agreed on in prayer. And not only does praying with another deepen our relationship with that person, but it also serves as a catalyst in prayer, while providing good accountability to stay in prayer.

Be accountable with someone and pray with them. Yet be careful to guard your time together so that it does not become a time when issues are discussed more than they are prayed for. Be sure to use this time to seek the Lord together.

Sometimes times of prayer with others can grow into larger groups, with many people involved. As it does, the following are some suggestions that are helpful to keep in mind.

Practical Suggestions for Prayer Groups

In prayer times, please *be careful to avoid the entertainment trap.*

Man likes to keep things busy and moving. By nature we are people who cannot sit still. It is hard to be quiet. We like pictures and slides. We like to have variety. We don't want anybody falling asleep or getting bored. Therefore, we keep so many things happening that we lose the quietness, the soberness, the intensity, the meditation and the devoutness that should be present in prayer. The sacredness of being in the holy of holies, sitting before God and gazing upon Him as we share our burdens with Him can easily be lost in the busyness and show of conducting a prayer meeting.

It is far too easy to get lost in the entertainment trap and deceive ourselves, thinking because since it felt like such an alive prayer meeting, it was productive. Unless we make sure we are listening to Him and following His lead, the Lord may be saying, "I waited for you to be quiet and open your heart to Me, but you wouldn't. You were so busy following the program that you missed Me. You talked to each other, but you didn't talk to Me; you didn't even listen to Me. There was no time when I could share My concerns with you."

I pray that this will not be so of us. We need organization, plans and agendas. Prayer meetings must not be dull. Involvement and participation are needed. But please, in the midst of all this, let us not miss the Lord. Let it be the Lord who stirs the prayer meeting and calls us to participate.

Also, we need to be sure to *guard our minds against wandering thoughts.*

Do you ever find that when somebody is praying and you start entering into prayer, all of a sudden your focus is gone? Your brain is on what happened during the day or some other random thought. But somehow, just before the end of the prayer, you snap back. You're able to say, "Amen," as though you were fully alert through the whole prayer.

Somehow, right after someone starts praying, within two or three sentences, I can be gone if I don't harness my thoughts. There are so many concerns, so much to do, so many calls I need to make that I can quickly lose focus in prayer. The enemy seeks to distract us like that so the promise "if two of you agree" (see Matthew 18:19) will be defeated.

Second Corinthians 10:5 speaks of this battle for our thoughts. It says, "Casting down arguments and every high thing that exalts itself against the knowledge of God, bringing every thought into captivity to the obedience of Christ."

Thousands of times my thoughts wander away in prayer. Maybe I am discouraged or depressed. Maybe I am thinking about what to do next. Many times I fail miserably. But then somehow, by God's grace, I'm able to catch hold of what is happening. Through the blood of Jesus and the Word, we can defeat the enemy and bring our thoughts into captivity. But we must be on the alert, ready to harness those thoughts and bring them into captivity to obey Christ.

In prayer meetings, *be sure to let liberty reign.*

We should have freedom to be the people God has created us to be. We should have freedom to express His thoughts with the emotion He gives us.

I remember attending a prayer meeting in South Korea a couple of years ago. I'd like to go back to Korea just for that experience again. Their culture is particularly a shame-culture; that is, they do not want to do anything to bring shame upon themselves or their family. But when it comes to prayer, these people are completely unashamed. They cry out to God in their loudest voice, with streams of tears running down every face.

We must learn to have liberty to be who God created us to be and act accordingly. Our God is the God of the quiet and the calm, as well as the God of the high-energy and expressive. I'm not trying to put everybody into one box. But there should be freedom to be joyful or exuberant. There should be freedom to express pain or sorrow. Tears, like Hannah's (see 1 Samuel 1), should not be quenched or misunderstood. We should not be intimidated into acting a certain way in our prayers.

We must also *watch out for too much regulation and too much control in prayer meetings.*

Those leading the prayer meeting should not be in total control of every second. It is not good to have someone tell you what to pray for and how to pray for it. It is not good to have to stop praying because somebody's watch said it was a certain time. We need to be led by the Holy Spirit.

There are times when we may not have any agenda in our times of prayer. And then at other times we may have many things on our agenda. In each case, let God's burden be given to us so that we will intercede for the things that are on His heart. Let us pray according to His will and His time frame.

At the same time, let us also *be on guard against having too little regulation, order or discipline.*

Sometimes prayer meetings can get out of hand if there is no framework or organization. Things can get crazy. We must avoid this because the devil can take control of these types of things. Prayer meetings can have these two extremes: There can be too much regulation so that people have no freedom, or there can be lack of any organization so that things are manipulated by the enemy. We need balance in this area.

But finally, *the most important thing is that you pray!* As you pray, the Lord will show you more of His heart in prayer and what He desires from you.

Concluding Remarks

I want to encourage you to pray. The opportunity to turn nations upside down is within our reach. But to do that God must go before us. Prayer lets God go before us. It acknowledges our dependence on Him for everything and exalts Him as Lord. This is an incredible time in which we live. It is a time for God to work and for us to see the kingdom's work established. It is a time for us to pray.

Prayer

Lord, draw us near to You in prayer. Protect and direct our prayer times. Guard our thoughts from wandering. Help us to draw near to Your heart so that we can hear Your concerns. Help us to pray always in Your will, not for our own self-ish desires. Give us Your burdens and then give us perseverance and patience to present our petitions. And Lord, thank You for Your example and Your joy in all of this. In Jesus' name. Amen.

If this booklet has been a blessing to you, I would really like to hear from you. You may write to Gospel for Asia, 1800 Golden Trail Court, Carrollton, TX 75010. Or send an email to kp@gfa.org.

Notes

Chapter 1

[1] Paul E. Billheimer, *Destined for the Throne* (Fort Washington, PA: CLC Publishers, 1975), p. 51.

Chapter 2

[1] Bill Adler, *Dear Lord* (Nashville, TN: Thomas Nelson, 1982).

[2] E.M. Bounds, *The Complete Works of E.M. Bounds on Prayer* (Grand Rapids, MI: Baker Book House, 1990), p. 231.

[3] Francois Fenelon, quoted in *The Tale of the Tardy Oxcart* by Charles R. Swindoll (Nashville, TN: W Publishing Group, 1998), p. 309.

Chapter 3

[1] E.M. Bounds, *The Complete Works of E.M. Bounds on Prayer*, p. 375.

[2] *Ibid.*, p. 309.

Chapter 4

[1] E.M. Bounds, *The Complete Works of E. M. Bounds on Prayer*, p. 227.

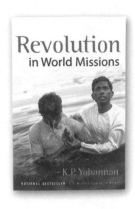

Instill
. . . a passion for the lost.

Impart
. . . fresh zeal for New
Testament living.

Stamp
. . . eternity on your eyes.

If you've been blessed by the insight K.P. Yohannan has shared through this booklet, you will want to read *Revolution in World Missions*, his first and most popular book.

When We Have Failed—What Next?

The best *is* yet to come. Do you find that hard to believe? If failure has clouded your vision to see God's redemptive power, this booklet is for you. God's ability to work out His best plan for your life remains. Believe it. (88 pages)

Order online at www.gfa.org

or call 1-800-WIN-ASIA

in Canada 1-888-WIN-ASIA

Booklets by K.P. Yohannan

A Life of Balance
Remember learning how to ride a bike? It was all a matter of balance. The same is true for our lives. Learn how to develop that balance, which will keep your life and ministry healthy and honoring God. (80 pages)

Dependence upon the Lord
Don't build in vain. Learn how to daily depend upon the Lord—whether in the impossible or the possible—and see your life bear lasting fruit. (48 pages)

Journey with Jesus
Take this invitation to walk the roads of life intimately with the Lord Jesus. Stand with the disciples and learn from Jesus' example of love, humility, power and surrender. (56 pages)

Learning to Pray
Whether you realize it or not, your prayers change things. Be hindered no longer as K.P. Yohannan shares how you can grow in your daily prayer life. See for yourself how God still does the impossible through prayer. (64 pages)

Living by Faith, Not by Sight
The promises of God are still true today: *"Anything is possible to him who believes!"* This balanced teaching will remind you of the power of God and encourage you to step out in childlike faith. (56 pages)

Principles in Maintaining a Godly Organization
Remember the "good old days" in your ministry? This book-let provides a biblical basis for maintaining that vibrancy and commitment that accompany any new move of God. (48 pages)

Seeing Him
Do you often live just day-to-day, going through the routine of life? We so easily lose sight of Him who is our everything. Through this booklet, let the Lord Jesus restore your heart and eyes to see Him again. (48 pages)

Stay Encouraged
How are you doing? Discouragement can sneak in quickly and subtly, through even the smallest things. Learn how to stay encouraged in every season of life, no matter what the circumstances may be. (56 pages)

That They All May Be One
In this booklet, K.P. Yohannan opens up his heart and shares from past struggles and real-life examples on how to maintain unity with those in our lives. A must read! (56 pages)

The Beauty of Christ through Brokenness
We were made in the image of Christ that we may reflect all that He is to the hurting world around us. Rise above the things that hinder you from doing this, and see how your life can display His beauty, power and love. (72 pages)

The Lord's Work Done in the Lord's Way
Tired? Burned out? Weary? The Lord's work done in His way will never destroy you. Learn what it means to minister unto Him and keep the holy love for Him burning strong even in the midst of intense ministry. A must-read for every believer! (72 pages)

The Way of True Blessing
What does God value most? Find out in this booklet as K.P. Yohannan reveals truths from the life of Abraham, an ordinary man who became the friend of God. (56 pages)

When We Have Failed—What Next?
The best *is* yet to come. Do you find that hard to believe? If failure has clouded your vision to see God's redemptive power, this booklet is for you. God's ability to work out His best plan for your life remains. Believe it. (88 pages)